THIS BOOK BELONGS TO

_____

M000111504

PRESIDENT THOMAS JEFFERSON HAD A FAVORITE MOCKINGBIRD NAMED DICK. HE WOULD SIT ON A TABLE AND SING AS THE PRESIDENT PLAYED THE VIOLIN.

THE MARQUIS DE LAFAYETTE BROUGHT AN ALLIGATOR ALONG WHEN HE CAME TO VISIT PRESIDENT JOHN QUINCY ADAMS. IT STAYED IN THE EAST ROOM.

PRESIDENT ABRAHAM LINCOLN'S FAMILY HAD MANY PETS. INCLUDING JACK - A TURKEY ORIGINALLY INTENDED TO BE SERVED AT A WHITE HOUSE DINNER.

PRESIDENT ANDREW JOHNSON GAVE FOOD AND WATER TO HIS LITTLE "PETS" - THE MICE HE FOUND IN HIS ROOM IN THE WHITE HOUSE.

PRESIDENT BENJAMIN HARRISON BOUGHT A GOAT NAMED "OLD WHISKERS" FOR HIS GRANDCHILDREN WHO WOULD RIDE IN THE LITTLE CART IT PULLED.

PRESIDENT WILLIAM MCKINLEY'S YELLOW-HEADED PARROT, NAMED "WASHINGTON POST," WOULD CHATTER TO EVERYONE WHO PASSED BY HIS PERCH.

WHEN PRESIDENT THEODORE ROOSEVELT'S SON ARCHIE WAS SICK, HIS BROTHERS USED THE WHITE HOUSE ELEVATOR TO BRING HIS PONY ALGONQUIN UP TO HIM IN HIS ROOM.

PRESIDENT HOWARD TAFT'S PERSONAL MILK COW "PAULINE WAYNE" USED TO GRAZE ON THE GRASS IN FRONT OF THE OLD EXECUTIVE BUILDING, WHICH IS NEXT TO THE WHITE HOUSE.

PRESIDENT WOODROW WILSON USED SHEEP AND THIS RAM NAMED
IKE TO TRIM THE WHITE HOUSE LAWN WHILE THE GARDENERS
SERVED IN WORLD WAR I.

PRESIDENT WARREN G. HARDING HAD A SPECIAL CHAIR MADE FOR HIS DOG "LADDIE BOY" TO SIT IN AT WHITE HOUSE MEETINGS.

PRESIDENT AND MRS. CALVIN COOLIDGE KEPT MANY UNUSUAL
ANIMALS AS PETS AT THE WHITE HOUSE, AND ONE OF THEIR
FAVORITES WAS REBECCA THE RACCOON.

WHEN AN OPOSSUM WANDERED ONTO WHITE HOUSE GROUNDS, PRESIDENT HERBERT HOOVER ALLOWED A SCHOOL BASEBALL TEAM TO ADOPT IT AS THEIR MASCOT.

PRESIDENT FRANKLIN DELANO ROOSEVELT OFTEN TOOK HIS SCOTTISH TERRIER FALA ALONG FOR A RIDE IN HIS CONVERTIBLE.

DURING PRESIDENT JOHN F. KENNEDY'S ADMINISTRATION, "MACARONI THE PONY" COULD OFTEN BE SEEN WANDERING AROUND THE WHITE HOUSE GROUNDS.

WHEN PRESIDENT LYNDON JOHNSON MOVED INTO THE WHITE HOUSE, HE HAD A SPECIAL DOGHOUSE BUILT FOR "HIM" AND "HER" THE FAMILY'S TWO BEAGLES.

PRESIDENT RICHARD NIXON'S FAMILY BROUGHT PASHA AND VICKY WITH THEM TO THE WHITE HOUSE, AND HIS STAFF GAVE HIM HIS OWN DOG WHICH HE NAMED "KING TIMAHOE."

PRESIDENT GERALD FORD USED TO INVITE LIBERTY, HIS GOLDEN RETRIEVER, TO LIE DOWN NEXT TO HIS DESK IN THE OVAL OFFICE.

A SIAMESE CAT NAMED "MISTY MALARKY YING YANG" MOVED INTO THE WHITE HOUSE WITH PRESIDENT JIMMY CARTER AND HIS FAMILY.

PRESIDENT RONALD REAGAN GAVE HIS WIFE NANCY A KING CHARLES SPANIEL FOR CHRISTMAS. SHE NAMED HIM REX.

TO PREPARE FOR MILLIE TO HAVE PUPPIES, PRESIDENT GEORGE H. W. BUSH'S WIFE BARBARA SET UP A "NESTING BOX" WITH NEWSPAPER SCRAPS AND A NEEDLEPOINT PILLOW.

PRESIDENT WILLIAM JEFFERSON CLINTON'S FAMILY PETS WERE
BUDDY THE DOG AND SOCKS THE CAT.

PRESIDENT GEORGE W. BUSH'S DOG SPOT WAS BORN AT THE WHITE HOUSE. SHE WAS ONE OF MILLIE'S PUPPIES.

PRESIDENT BARACK OBAMA AND HIS FAMILY ADOPTED BO, A PORTUGUESE WATER DOG, IN 2009, THEIR FIRST YEAR LIVING IN THE WHITE HOUSE.